TABLE OF CONTENTS

DISCLAIMER AND TERMS OF USE AGREEMENT:

Introduction – Bias, Emotion, & Overconfidence

Chapter 1 - Laying A Proper Foundation

Chapter 2 – Perception Investing

Chapter 3 – Noise Trader Theory

Chapter 4 - Efficient Market Hypothesis (EMH)

Chapter 5 – Summary & Conclusions

I Have a Special Gift for My Readers

Meet the Author

Bias, Emotion, & Overconfidence
The True Story Behind Behavioral Finance & Investing
©Copyright 2013 by Dr. Leland Benton

DISCLAIMER AND TERMS OF USE AGREEMENT:

(Please Read This Before Using This Book)

This information is for educational and informational purposes only. The content is not intended to be a substitute for any professional advice, diagnosis, or treatment.

The author and publisher of this book and the accompanying materials have used their best efforts in preparing this book.

The author and publisher make no representation or warranties with respect to the accuracy, applicability, fitness, or completeness of the contents of this book. The information contained in this book is strictly for educational purposes. Therefore, if you wish to apply ideas contained in this book, you are taking full responsibility for your actions.

The author and publisher disclaim any warranties (express or implied), merchantability, or fitness for any particular purpose. The author and publisher shall in no event be held liable to any party for any direct, indirect, punitive, special, incidental or other consequential damages arising directly or indirectly from any use of this material, which is provided "as is", and without warranties. As always, the advice of a competent legal, tax, accounting, medical or other professional should be sought where applicable.

The author and publisher do not warrant the performance, effectiveness or applicability of any sites listed or linked to in this book. All links are for information purposes only and are not warranted for content, accuracy or any other implied or explicit purpose. No part of this may be copied, or changed in any format, or used in any way other than what is outlined within this course under any circumstances. Violators will be prosecuted.

This book is © Copyrighted by ePubWealth.com.

Introduction – Bias, Emotion, & Overconfidence

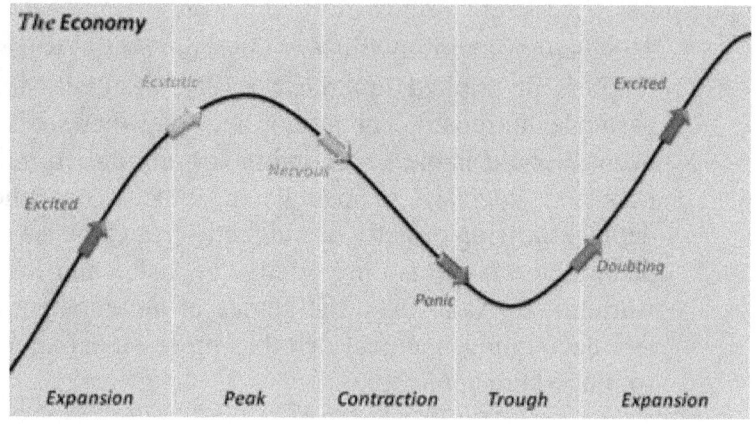

In this book, I am going to introduce you to the behavioral science behind the Bias, Emotion, & Overconfidence of finance and personal investing.

Even an amateur to the marketplace knows that Bias, Emotion, & Overconfidence run the markets worldwide. You are not going to get away from the investor emotions as it pertains to the worldwide markets and even with all of the computer models, technology and such that allows investors to make decisions, emotions will always drive investing worldwide.

Here is an article that describes exactly what I am talking about…

After Apple's Rise, a Bruising Fall

http://www.nytimes.com/2013/04/19/technology/after-apples-rise-a-bruising-fall.html?ref=business&nl=business&emc=edit_dlbkam_20130419

By NATHANIEL POPPER and NICK WINGFIELD

Wall Street has turned viciously on its one-time iDarling. The rout in Apple's share price — it fell nearly 2.7 percent on Thursday, bringing the damage since late September to 44 percent — has many wondering when, and where, all of this will end.

The answer, of course, is that no one really knows. Yes, Apple is slowing, as companies inevitably do. But Apple remains enormously profitable and the envy of corporations worldwide.

And yet Apple's decline in the stock market has been so swift and so brutal that the development has begun to change the way investors view the company. Apple no longer looks like a sure thing.

It is a remarkable turn in one of the standout stock market stories of recent years. Only seven months ago, Apple's share price raced above $700 to a record high, making Apple the most valuable company on the planet. By Thursday, the stock had sunk to $392.05, closing below $400 for the first time since late 2011.

The proximate cause of Thursday's decline was news this week of a glut of audio chips at one of Apple's suppliers. That, in turn, prompted concern that sales of iPhones might fall short of expectations.

But that was just one more bit of downbeat news in what has been a downbeat few months. All told, $290 billion has been wiped off Apple's value since September. It might seem difficult to believe, but Apple now ranks among the biggest losers in the stock market over the last seven months, right next to the J. C. Penney Company, that sick man of American department stores. The last time Apple was trading this low was in November 2011. Steve Jobs had just died and everyone wondered how Apple would carry on without its visionary leader.

Stock price aside, Apple is bigger and, by some measures, stronger today that it was then. It sells more iPhones and iPads than ever. It is expanding its global reach. And it is making so much money — analysts expect the company to report another solid quarter next week — that it has been having trouble figuring out what to do with all of its cash. Speculation is rife that Apple might pass some cash to shareholders in the form of an increased stock dividend.

On one level, the Apple story is a common one on Wall Street: what goes up also goes down. As Apple's stock price soared in recent years, some pointed out that the company's sales couldn't keep growing — and its share price couldn't keep rising — at that rapid pace forever. **In hindsight, Apple's surge above $700 strikes some as irrational, as does its precipitous plunge back below $400.**

"Overexuberance on the upside leads to herd behavior and panic during the correction," said

Avanidhar Subrahmanyam, a professor of behavioral finance at U.C.L.A. "People just panic and the stress hormone kicks in."

One issue is that Apple is a favorite stock among individual investors. The investment firm SigFig estimated last fall that 17 percent of all retail investors owned Apple stock, four times the number that owns the average stock in the Dow Jones industrial average.

Trading by retail investors can be amplified by hedge funds, which see everyday investors piling in and push in the opposite direction by shorting the stock, betting it will decline. The so-called short interest in Apple reached a peak last November, but hasn't gone down much since then, according to data from NASDAQ.

Aswath Damodaran, professor of finance at New York University, said the enthusiasm surrounding Apple last year prompted him to sell his own holdings in the company when the stock was around $610.

"I was terrified by the kinds of investors coming into Apple's stock," said Mr. Damodaran. "Not only were they coming in with unrealistic expectations, they were at war with each other."

Recently, Mr. Damodaran began buying shares again, convinced that the fears had gone too far.

"Right now, Apple is being priced as though it has no future growth," he said.

Indeed, Apple looks cheap by the most popular way of gauging a stock's value, the amount of profit it generates for each outstanding share. Investors are willing to pay about $15 for a dollar of profit of the average Standard & Poor's 500 company. But for Apple, they will pay less than $9.

News from the technology industry, including start-ups, the Internet, enterprise and gadgets. On Twitter: @nytimesbits.

At its current price, investors are betting that Apple will grow more slowly than the average American company. And they are ignoring the enormous pile of cash that Apple has built up, which it could hand out to shareholders tomorrow if it wanted.

The cash, and Apple's apparent inability to find a use for it, has taken some of the blame for the stock's recent performance.

Toni Sacconaghi, an analyst at Bernstein Research, said that if Apple developed a clear plan to use some of its cash to pay dividends to shareholders it would help the company's shares, perhaps lifting them 10 percent or more. But that will not return Apple shares to their glory days. He said the bigger problem bearish investors saw with Apple's shares was more straightforward: growth is stalling.

"That's the story," he said.

During the fiscal second quarter that Apple will report next Tuesday, Mr. Sacconaghi predicts that Apple will post an 18 percent decline in net income, as less lucrative products eat into its profit margins. In 2012 during that same period, Apple almost doubled its net income from the same period in 2011.

Still, this is Apple — the company that produces some of the most popular products in the world. While Mr. Jobs is no longer around, almost all the people who worked with him are still there.

One thing is sure: the shift in sentiment has been a big change for Apple bulls like Gene Munster, an analyst at Piper Jaffray. He still sees host of opportunities for growth ahead. He said that, for instance, Apple could play a big role in mobile payments.

But it's no longer easy being an Apple bull.

"It's like getting a beating every day coming into work," Mr. Munster said. "Investors are so negative; they want to take it out on somebody. I feel like I end up being that guy."

*****

Here is another article you will find interesting too…

One Man's Currency Is Another Man's Bet
By FLOYD NORRIS
http://www.nytimes.com/2013/04/19/business/gold-currency-to-some-is-acting-like-a-speculative-

commodity.html?ref=todayspaper&nl=business&emc=edit_dlbkam_20130419

Nicolas Asfouri/Agence France-Presse — Getty Images

Gold necklaces in Bangkok. Gold has some commercial uses, including jewelry, but to the faithful, it's money, not a commodity.

Multimedia

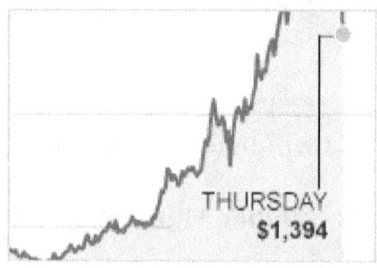

Price of Gold

The gold market, circa 2013.

In the more than four decades since President Richard M. Nixon severed the dollar's last ties to gold, there have been two bull markets in gold — markets that peaked not that far apart, when adjusted for inflation. To a believer, gold is different from any other commodity. The others are expected to rise and fall with supply and demand. A supply shock, perhaps caused by a drought in Brazil or a confrontation in the Persian Gulf, may send the price of orange juice or oil soaring. A fall in economic activity may depress the value of any industrial commodity. A commodity, like any other investment, can become overvalued or undervalued.

But to the faithful, that doesn't include gold. Sure, it has uses in the real economy, like jewelry and dentistry. But that is not the important issue. To them, it is money. It cannot be overvalued.

There was a time when gold really was money, when the gold standard reigned supreme. Its record was not an especially good one. There was the minor issue of supply shocks — as when gold from the New World caused drastic inflation in Spain — and there were repeated panics and depressions in the 19th century. A determination to stick to the gold standard helped worsen the Great Depression.

But to those who revere gold, such problems are minor compared to the sins of fiat money, which is defined as money not anchored in gold but instead determined by central bankers, who can — and eventually will — surrender to political pressures to devalue the currency. Discretion will be abused.

Those who back the gold standard think "you can design a rule that will tell you what to do, no matter what the circumstances," says Robert J. Barbera, the co-director of the Center for Financial Economics at Johns Hopkins University. "But there is no one-size-fits-all rule for monetary policy. Ultimately, you need discretion."

Central bankers go in and out of fashion. Back in the late 1970s and early 1980s, as inflation grew and grew in the United States and other developed economies, their credibility was challenged as never before. Gold, and its sort-of sibling, silver, soared, but then crashed back to earth well before Paul A. Volcker, then the chairman of the Federal Reserve, proved he could and would tame inflation, even if doing so sent the American economy into back-to-back recessions.

During January 1980, as the first of those recessions was beginning, gold went from a little over $500 an ounce to $850 and then back under $700.

By early 1999, when Time Magazine put the Federal Reserve chairman, Alan Greenspan, on its cover as the head of "the Committee to Save the World," central bankers had become geniuses. (The other members of that committee were the former Treasury secretary, Robert E. Rubin, and his deputy at the time, Lawrence H. Summers, who later succeeded Mr. Rubin.) The stock market was booming, recessions were distant memories and gold was under $300 an ounce.

After 1980, gold never got close to $800 an ounce until; once again, the central bankers began to look imperfect.

In 2007, as the American economy struggled to deal with what was then seen as the subprime housing crisis, gold climbed back above $800 and then set a new high, in nominal dollars, early in 2008, early in the American recession.

This time around, the sin of central banks appeared to be one of inadequate regulation, and of allowing a credit boom to get out of hand. If William McChesney Martin Jr., a former Fed chairman, once said the Fed's job was "to take away the punch bowl just when the party gets going," Mr. Greenspan was spiking the punch during his final years.

The hostility to the Fed since then has been largely based on worries that, Ben S. Bernanke, Mr. Greenspan's successor, was going to destroy the dollar. Having lowered short-term rates to virtually zero, the Fed and other central banks have purchased huge quantities of government bonds. That is not printing money in the sense that no printing press is involved, but in every other sense it is.

Surely, said those who believe in gold, burdensome inflation was just around the corner. The Republican platform in 2012 did not use the phrase "gold standard," but said "as we face the task of cleaning up the wreckage of the current administration's policies," a Republican administration would appoint a "commission to investigate possible ways to set a fixed value for the dollar."

By the time of the Republican convention, it turned out, gold had peaked at a little more than $1,900 an ounce. This week, in what looked like panic selling, the metal fell back below $1,400.

In 1980, as in this year, gold had attracted a lot of speculators who might or might not care about a gold standard, but who knew a rising market when they saw one. Exchange-traded funds have made it a lot easier to invest in gold — no need to store a gold bar or a bag of coins — and they have also made it much easier to borrow money to support such positions. Margin calls no doubt had something to do with Monday's plunge, as they did with the collapse of silver futures back in 1980.

In 1980, a case could be made that those margin calls, in the futures market, were brought on by a conspiracy against the people who had driven prices up. An article in Fortune Magazine: http://features.blogs.fortune.cnn.com/2011/05/08/who-guards-whom-at-the-commodity-exchange-fortune-1980/ pointed to changes in the rules at the commodity exchange, making it all but impossible to speculate on silver prices continuing to rise. This time, there are no obvious changes in rules to explain the plunge. **It may be that a lot of people simply placed bets with borrowed money, expecting a disaster that has not arrived, and now are scrambling to minimize their losses.**

Perhaps, as in 1980, evidence is growing that the central bankers are getting it right — or at least right enough. By coincidence, the day after the Monday plunge in gold, the International Monetary Fund released its World

Economic Report: http://www.imf.org/external/pubs/ft/weo/2013/01/, with a chapter titled "The dog that didn't bark: Has inflation been muzzled?" The chapter had a suitable quantity of "buts" and "howevers," but the basic answer was "Yes," in large part because people trust central bankers and assume that central bank inflation targets will be met, at least in the long run.

"Fears about high inflation should not prevent monetary authorities from pursuing highly accommodative monetary policy," the I.M.F. concluded.

It may be a coincidence, but this week's plunge coincided with growing publicity for a currency that sounds a little like gold, at least if you are not paying close attention. That is the digital currency called bitcoin, which has of late been more volatile than a dot-com stock in 1999. Invented in 2009, its supply supposedly is controlled by a rigid computer program, making it, like gold, not subject to central bank manipulation. It got an endorsement last week from The Economist magazine: "Regulators should keep their hands off new forms of digital money such as bitcoin," the magazine wrote, proclaiming that the bitcoin's "unique digital signature" makes it "impossible to forge."

To gold advocates, that kind of talk is dangerous.

"The bitcoin is not the answer to the Federal Reserve's depredations against the dollar," wrote Steve Forbes, a former presidential hopeful, in his blog at Forbes.com: http://www.forbes.com/sites/steveforbes/2013/04/16/bitc

oin-whatever-it-is-its-not-money/. "The basic reason: It has no fixed value. It trades like a stock or commodity. In recent days it has been crashing after a spectacular rise in terms of dollars. Such volatility makes it useless as a means to do transactions."

Of course, you could say something similar about gold.

*****

Okay, after reading these two articles it is easy to see the emotions behind the rise and fall of Apple stock and the price of gold.

Now let's me lay the foundation to this book by teaching you the behavioral science behind people's emotions and in turn behind behavioral investing.

Chapter 1 - Laying A Proper Foundation

In all of my "Why" series of books, I will provide the following discourse on the Human Mind in order to lay a proper foundation to what I am about to teach.

The Mechanism of the Human Mind

Which Comes First - the Body or the Mind?
(the most important concept in all of talk therapy)
© 2007, Steven Paglierani, The Center for Emergence

Understanding the Body - Mind Connection

For thousands of years, we have known there is a body – mind connection. Until now though, we have not known what this connection is. What it it? Time. The body and the mind each have their own sense of time. Their own clocks so to speak. Therapy works only when these two clocks are in sync.

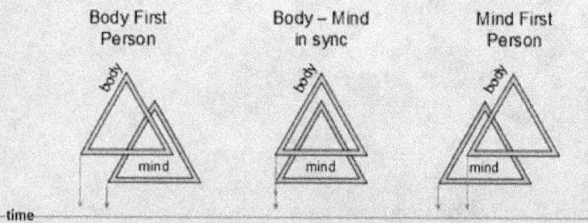

Prior to the fall of man into sin as described in the Garden of Eden, man's spirit was hooked to God's infinite spirit. There was no death because God's spirit is infinite. Man is the only animal on earth that shares the eternality nature of God. The subject of eternal life has been a heated topic of man from the beginning of our existence.

In Greek mythology, there's a story about a mortal youth named Tithonus. Aurora, the goddess of dawn, fell in love with the boy and when Zeus, the king of the gods, promised to grant Aurora any gift she chose for her lover, she asked that Tithonus might live forever. But, in her haste she forgot to ask for eternal youth, so when Zeus granted her request, Tithonus was doomed to an eternity of perpetual aging as a grouchy old man… forever.

In the movie "Highlander," Angus McLeod was born in 1518 as an immortal being. He could not die and to me, the best part of the movie was the depiction of this immortal's agony here on earth as he watched everything he loved die forcing him to begin his life over and over again. He saw all of the ugliness, which man had caused over four centuries. He witnessed the Spanish Inquisition, Waterloo, the atrocities of the Third Reich, and more. He saw the slavery and bigotry of the eighteenth century, the slaughter of the Native American tribes after the Civil War. This man's life was a living Hell!

There is a very big difference between the ways our feeble minds picture eternal life versus God's idea of eternal life. Our understanding comes from Quantum Physics and is limited within the Time-Space Continuum.

Life is your spirit, but the soul of man has usurped the spirit's position and psychology is now forced to define "how" we live our lives based on the animating force of the soul instead of the spirit. As I said previously, the soul has usurped the spirit's place as our animating force. Let's discuss this now.

- ❖ **Body First Person** - When the body becomes our life, we live as animals.
- ❖ **Body-Mind In Sync** - When the soul becomes our life, we live as rebels and fugitives in a life of desires, emotions, and will (consuming entities). This is the position of mankind today!
- ❖ **Mind First Person** - But when we come to live our life in the mind/spirit and by the spirit, though we still use our soul's faculties just as we do our physical faculties, they are now the servants of the spirit.

If you live as a consuming entity, you will always lose. In other words, to get, you must give - you must sacrifice! Have you ever wondered why you have so many anxieties, phobias, worries and fears? The reality of this world is evil. So what is reality? I will tell you. This is reality:

"Life without war is impossible either in nature or in grace. The basis of physical, mental, moral and spiritual life is antagonism. Health is the balance between physical life and external nature, and it is maintained only by sufficient vitality on the inside against things on the outside. Everything outside my physical life is designed to put me to death. Things, which keep me going when I am alive, disintegrate me when I am dead. If I have enough fighting power, I produce the balance of health.

The same is true of mental life. If I want to maintain a vigorous mental life, I have to fight, and in that way the mental balance called thought is produced. Morally it is the same. Everything that does not partake of the nature of virtue is the enemy of virtue in me, and it depends on what moral caliber I have whether I overcome and produce virtue (GOOD CHARACTER). Immediately I fight, I am moral in that particular. No man is virtuous because he cannot help it; virtue (character) is acquired.

- ❖ Psychology only studies the observable aspects of the mind and discounts the unseen or intangible aspects of the human mind.
- ❖ Behavioral science attempts to study the intangible aspects of the human mind…why you do the things you do and more importantly why you don't do what you should do.
- ❖ There is no such thing as commercial psychology versus personal psychology. The mind uses the same mechanism to evaluate all types of relationships.
- ❖ Everything we do revolves around relationships. We relate to our environment, our friends, family, co-workers, other people and even our pets. We are social animals.

The Mechanism of the Human Mind

Belief Systems + Thought + Delight = Action/Behavior/Conduct

Conscious Mind

5-senses:
Sight
Hearing
Taste
Touch
Smell
ESP (women only)

Subconscious Mind

Intellect:
Experiential
Empirical

DEW:
Desires, Emotions and Will

The Human Psyche Differences Between Genders

The female psyche operates on emotional, spiritual, physical and intellectual planes
The male psyche operates only on the intellectual and physical planes.

Here is an exercise you might find weird but it demonstrates the power of the human mind.

Fi yuo cna raed tihs, yuo hvae a sgtrane mnid too. Cna yuo raed tihs? Olny 55 plepoe out of 100 can. I cdnuolt blveiee taht I cluod aulaclty uesdnatnrd waht I was rdanieg. The phaonmneal pweor of the hmuan

mnid, aoccdrnig to a rscheearch at Cmabrigde Uinervtisy, it dseno't mtaetr in waht oerdr the ltteres in a wrod are, the olny iproamtnt tihng is taht the frsit and lsat ltteer be in the rghit pclae. The rset can be a taotl mses and you can sitll raed it whotuit a pboerlm. Tihs is bcuseae the huamn mnid deos not raed ervey lteter by istlef, but the wrod as a wlohe. Azanmig huh? Yaeh and I awlyas tghuhot slpeling was ipmorantt!

You might have found it somewhat unusual that you could probably read the jumbled mess above. Actually over half the people that see this exercise can decipher the words at the same speed of reading as if the words were not jumbled.

It is important to note that the human mind thinks in packages...concepts rather than individual ideas.

Your eyes see each letter but the mind looks at the whole word instead. As you read, the mind looks at the first and last letter only. Remember this; the mind sees the beginning and end. We will talk about this later...

If you were to listen to an orchestra, your ear listens to every note from every instrument but a trained ear can actually pick out individual instruments from the whole sound as the mind hears the whole symphony.

How does this apply to you?

Learning to observe means going beyond the mind's natural ability to only read the first and last letters of a word!

It is training the mind to see all the letters, not just the eye but the mind!

Truisms About the Human Mind

- Pain vs. Pleasure – people are more motivated to avoid pain than seek pleasure.
- A person that is suffering depression will seek relief (notice I didn't say cure) before they seek happiness.
- The human mind cannot tell the difference between fantasy and reality.
- The human mind gravitates to the desires, emotions and will of its psyche. People crave entertainment so fantasy dominates their existences.
- The human mind is easily distracted! You can either be the cause of these distractions or other stimuli will be the cause but rest assured people WILL BE distracted because the human mind is gullible.

The human mind responds quickly to these three forms of stimuli

- Sex
- Humor
- FEAR

But the greatest of them all is FEAR!

BTW – on the positive side we have faith, hope, love, but the greatest of these *is* LOVE.

Fear usually takes the form of what is called "Scarcity Thought"

You are afraid that someone will have what you feel belongs to you or that others will have more "stuff" than you.

- ❖ The subconscious mind is often referred to as the "heart," and is the control mechanism the body uses to store our beliefs.

- ❖ **These beliefs are stored as pictures in our "hearts" and create frequencies in our bodies.**

- ❖ We know that the optimum human frequency is a little below 7.83 hertz. To drop below this frequency brings on the onslaught of disease. To rise above it a person demonstrates psychic abilities.

- ❖ Harmful beliefs that cause unhealthy frequencies are the source of almost all problems - physical, mental, emotional.

- ❖ The subconscious mind creates a belief system, which we call "pictures of the heart."

- ❖ These pictures involve either visions, or dreams/fantasies.

- ❖ Science has discovered that the subconscious mind cannot distinguish between fantasy and reality.

*The subject of all dreams is the dreamer.
*Dreams are born in our desires, emotions and will.
*Dreamers believe in a belief system, which is fantasy.
*A life lived within a fantasy creates a feeling of self-centeredness, hopelessness and despair. In dreams everything is perfect.
*The subject of a vision is not the visionary but the world.
*Visions are born in the intellect.
*Visions are pictures of the future that have already been experienced in the heart of those who give it birth.
*Visionaries sacrifice themselves for the good of mankind.
*Visions have a moral quality that transcends the self-centered nature of dreams.
*By its very nature a vision launches a mission, a "cause-that-inspires."
*Visions create a sense of belonging.

- ❖ We act upon visions and/or dreams, using thought.
- ❖ Thought employs the intellect, in the case of visions, or the desires, emotions and the will, in the case of dreams.
- ❖ Intellectual thought relies on wisdom; emotional thought relies on the pursuit of pleasure, comfort and delight.
- ❖ Dreamers live within a facade; they create a false sense of worth using imaginary situations.

- ❖ Visionaries live within reality; they create change, within a framework of restraint, and intellectual thought.
- ❖ The world is made up of OPPOSITES, which is usually the corrupted version of the original. We have good and evil. We have love and lust!
- ❖ EVERYTHING YOU DO IS BECAUSE OF LOVE OR LUST. Learn to love because there are no crimes beyond forgiveness.

*Love is born in the intellect; lust is born in the DEW!
*Love is vision; lust is fantasy.
*Love restrains & sacrifices; lust is selfish
*Love is being one with someone or something
*Lust is being with someone or something.
*Visionaries love; dreamers lust!
*Visionaries do what is required; dreamers just do their best!

WHEN THERE IS NO HOPE OF LOVE DO WE ABANDON OURSELVES TO LUST?

Yes we do!

Pictures of the heart are your belief system.

- ❖ We animate these pictures into either fantasies, or visions.
- ❖ People do not appear to see the difference between the matter part of an organism and the life part, which animates it.

- ❖ We seem to think that the organism itself is life. In other words, it is not our outward appearance that is our life, but our inward existence.
- ❖ Life is what goes into the body. Death is what comes out.
- ❖ A person who lies is not a liar because he tells a lie. The lie is the manifested behavior of some subconscious belief system. The lie only demonstrates that the person is a liar…it is the effect.
- ❖ Except for love, the power of words inspired by a vision or fantasy is the most potent human force.

"Do you want to have or do you want to be?"

*For a dreamer: "Seeing is believing!"
*But they only see imaginary things that are not real!!
*This is why "The Secret" is WRONG!
*Say it and claim it is WRONG!
*Blab it and grab it IS WRONG!
*See it and be it IS WRONG!
Dreamers practice companionship – To be with someone or something!

VERY IMPORTANT:

1. Dreamers covet the object of their temptation, BUT they covet <u>the temptation</u> more so than <u>the object</u> itself because <u>the temptation is the idol of their fantasy</u>.
2. If there is a conflict between the conscious and subconscious mind, the subconscious mind always wins…ALWAYS!

3. All reaction occurs in the conscious mind; all interaction occurs in the subconscious mind. Fear is a "REACTION" to losing control.

For a visionary: "Believing is seeing!"

There are no SECRETS; there are only challenges to be conquered!

THIS IS NOT A SECRET: Putting a photo of a Ferrari on your refrigerator and seeing yourself driving it by employing the so-called law of attraction is pure BUPKES!!! Why? Because this is all occurring in the conscious mind and beliefs reside in the subconscious mind. How do you transfer something from the conscious mind to the subconscious mind and make it a belief system?

A Ferrari is the object of your temptation but what you covet most is the temptation of owning a Ferrari because the temptation is the idol of your fantasy.

It is all about ATTENTION & ACCEPTANCE!!!!! I have a $100 bill in my hand and I am willing to give it to you. But if you don't ACCEPT it then it is still in my hand. BELIEF SYSTEMS ARE CREATED BY ATTENTION & ACCEPTANCE!

John 1:12 But as many as received him, to them gave he **the right** to become children of God, *even* to them that believe on his name

Human things must be known to be loved; but divine things must be loved to be known.

BELIEVING IS SEEING!

Let's talk about goals…which of the following goals are good goals?

- ❖ To want to get married and have a wonderful, happy, loving marriage?
- ❖ To want to have children who are happy, successful, and loving?
- ❖ To have a successful, fulfilling and rewarding career?
- ❖ Is it a good goal to want to have fun, bonded, loving, and meaningful relationships with other people?

Which of the listed goals are good goals? None of them!

You should never have anything for a goal that is not 100% under your control, AND each and every goal should be <u>motivated by love</u>.

Almost all goals that we have in our life are wrong.

Everything that we do, we do because of a goal we have.

When we get up in the morning, it's because of some goal that we have; we are hungry for breakfast, or we need to go to work.

If we go to the grocery store, it's because of some goal we have. If we are kind to people, it's because of some goal that we have.

Now we don't always know what they are, because a lot of these are subconscious goals.

The goals we have are the reasons for everything we do. But, do all of your goals involve only YOU?

Of course not!

And when the other person, or persons, in your goal do not perform, or act the way you want them to, then we become anxious and stressed.

When our goals get blocked, it creates anger, anxiety, and frustration. If we only have good goals, we will not experience anger or anxiety.

That's how you know, if you are living a wrongful goal. If the result is anger and frustration because your control was blocked and blocking your goal, then you had a wrongful goal. It may have been a fine and noble desire, but a wrongful goal.

Filters
We live in a society of consumerism and entertainment. In my previous books I have spoken reams about this subject. Instant gratification is paramount and today's technology delivers information and other stimuli in bucketfuls to the human mind. We have already spoken about filters that the human mind employs to weed out

what it determines to be irrelevant. This "irrelevancy" is different in every individual and many times is programmed into our minds subconsciously or without us knowing it. We have also spoken about the causes of these various filters such as environment, maturity, upbringing, culture, etc.

The one essential common element of all filters is that they are all ATTENTION diverters. We have spoken about attention earlier; what is very interesting is that filters are generally viewed as bad when some are really very good.

I had a friend, who lives in Chicago, fall on hard times and needed assistance. When I got to him he was living in a cheap hotel and had a room so small when you put the key in the door you broke the *window (I slay me)*. His room was about 50 feet from the Loop (the overhead train that circles around Chicago). The noise was deafening when the train went by, and it went by often, but my friend had filtered it out. Amazing, but when you thing about it, my friend really does hear the train but yet he pays no attention to it, so in actuality, it is like he doesn't hear it at all! So filters divert attention, and take away our focus; so let's talk about focus.

The Incredible Power of Focus
One of the more important points I have made has been the idea that you really do create your own life and your own reality. I know this idea has become a kind of personal growth cliché that many of us have heard over and over for years. Many people, after continuing to experience the same old ups and downs and personal dramas over many years, get to the point where they dismiss this idea as charming but useless -- or just plain

wrong. "If I'm creating this, then I'm certainly not doing it on purpose," they say. "It sure seems like this is HAPPENING to me, rather than that I'm creating it." They just assume that it's all BS because "this and this and this and this are going on for me, and I have no control over it, and anyone who thinks I'm creating this doesn't understand what I'm going through." Essentially, they are resigning themselves to becoming a victim of circumstances.

We live in a universe of infinite complexity and many forces -- way too many to keep track of -- operate on us. Yes, it is true that we are NOT in control of everything that happens, because we are not in control of most of those infinite other parts of the universe. In fact, the only thing you have total and complete control over is...YOUR OWN MIND. That is, if you learn how to exercise it.

Luckily, this one thing -- your mind -- that you do have control over gives you tremendous power. By exercising control over your mind, you can get the rest of those infinite other parts of the universe to begin to march in formation.

The person who says, "If I'm creating this, it certainly isn't on purpose," is right. They are not creating what is happening to them "on purpose." Who would purposely create failure, or bad relationships, or any other kind of suffering? You can only do something that is not good for you that is harmful to you, if you do it subconsciously. This means if you are creating something you don't want, you must be doing so subconsciously.

Your mind is running on automatic pilot, based on "software" (subconscious programming) installed when you were too young to know any better, by parents, teachers, friends, the media, and other experiences and influences. The key is to become more conscious, more aware...to get yourself off automatic pilot. Once you do this, you stop creating all the dramas and other garbage you don't want in your life.

How do you do this? One way is by remembering and using a very important piece of wisdom. What is this important piece of wisdom? I'm glad you asked.

It's the fact that whatever you focus on manifests as reality in your life.

You are always focusing on something, whether you are aware of it or not. If I spent some time with you, and heard your history, I could tell you what you are focusing on. How? By looking at the results you are getting in your life. The results you get are always the result of your focus.

The problem is this focus is usually not conscious focus; it's automatic or subconscious focus. We subconsciously focus on something we don't want, and then when we get it we feel like a victim and don't even stop to think that we created it in the first place. And what is more, we don't realize we could choose to create something completely different if we could only get out of the cycle of subconsciously focusing on something other than what we want.

If you have a significant negative emotional experience (say, for instance, a relationship in which you are abused or mistreated in some way), a part of you is going to say: "Okay, I get it. There are people out there who can and will hurt me. Relationships can be dangerous and painful. I have to watch out for these people [or sometimes, relationships in general] and avoid them." Unfortunately, to watch out for them and avoid them, you have to focus your mind on "people who could hurt me," or "bad relationships," and that focus draws more of what you don't want to you...AND...actually makes these things you don't want (at least initially) attractive to you, so when they appear in your life you are drawn to them. This is why many people keep having one relationship after another with the same person, but in different bodies. This, of course, applies to everything, not just relationships. I'm just using relationships as an example.

Focusing on what you do not want, ironically, makes it happen. Focusing on not being poor makes you poor. Focusing on not making mistakes causes you to make mistakes. Focusing on not having a bad relationship creates bad relationships. Focusing on not being depressed makes you depressed. Focusing on not smoking makes you want to smoke. And so on. I think you get the idea. The mind will create what you focus on both GOOD and BAD!!!

The truth is your mind cannot tell the difference between something you think about or focus on that you DO want, and something you think about or focus on but do NOT want. The mind is a goal-seeking mechanism, and an extremely effective one at that. Already, all the time, it is elegantly and precisely creating exactly what you focus on. You are already a World Champion Expert at creating whatever you focus on. You couldn't get any better at it, and you don't need to get any better at it.

When you focus on anything, your mind says: "Okay, we can do that," and starts figuring out how to do it. It doesn't ask whether you're focusing on it because you want it or because you do not want it. It ALWAYS assumes you want what you focus on and then it goes and makes it happen. The more frequent and the more intense the focus, the faster and more completely you will create what you have focused on, which is why intense negative experiences create intense focus on what you do not want, and tend to make you re-create what you don't want, over and over.

Most of the time, for most people, all the focusing and thinking is going by at warp speed, on automatic, without much, if any, conscious intention. Your job is to learn how to direct this power by consciously directing your focus to the outcomes you want. Once you do, everything changes. This does, however, take some work, because at first you have to swim upstream against the current of your old, unconscious habits, and the current can be swift and strong. Trained observation actually teaches you to focus on what you want.

First, you have to discover all the things you focus on that you do not want, and I'm willing to bet there are quite a few -- way more than you think. To the degree you're getting what you don't want, you are focusing, albeit subconsciously, on what you don't want.

Spend some time over the next few weeks making a list of all the things you do NOT want as you notice yourself thinking about them.

Second, you have to get very clear about what you DO want. Then, you have to examine each of the things you want and be sure they are not just something you do NOT want in disguise. For instance, saying "I want a relationship where I am treated well" would not even be an issue if you had not had relationships where you were not treated well, and even in making this seemingly positive statement you are focusing on not wanting to be mistreated. Saying "I want a reliable car" wouldn't even come up if you weren't focusing on the fact that you don't want a car that breaks down and needs a lot of repairs.

After you've sorted out the things you habitually focus on that you do not want, and know what you do want, you have to begin to notice each time you think about an outcome you do not want, and consciously change your thinking, right in that moment, so you are instead focusing on what you do want.

Remember, you do NOT have to avoid things to be happy and get what you want. The urge to avoid something is a result of having had a negative emotional experience regarding that thing, and trying to avoid things requires you to focus on them, which tells your brain to create them. Not good.

You will be surprised how often you are thinking about what you do not want, how difficult it is to catch yourself doing it every time, and -- most of all – how difficult it is to switch your thinking to what you DO want. There is a strong momentum to keep thinking about that thing you want to avoid. As I said, the current is strong and swift, especially at first.

The solution? Practice, practice, practice. Persistence, persistence, persistence!!!

It's a very good idea to write down what you want, very specifically, so that your Fairy Godmother, were she to read it, would know exactly what to give you without any additional explanation.

Then, read what you have written to yourself, preferably out loud, several times a day, while seeing yourself, in your mind, already having what you want.

Believing is seeing and not the other way around as the world teaches you!

The more emotion you can bring to it, the better. Then, take whatever action is available to begin moving toward what you want. A good time to do this reading and visualizing is when you first wake up and before you go to bed.

I know this is work. Do it anyway. There is a price for everything, and this is the price you must pay to get what you want. Be prepared to pay it. It will be worth it, I promise. And be prepared to pay for a while before you get results. Stick with it.

Another way to change your focus is to ask questions. As an example, I'll ask you one right now. What did you have for breakfast this morning? To answer this question (even to just internally process the question), you had to shift your focus from whatever your mind was focused on (hopefully, to what I am teaching) to today's breakfast.

This means that to change your focus, all you have to do is...ask yourself a question!

It also means you better be careful what questions you ask yourself. Good questions include "How can I get X?" "How can I do X?" "How can I be X?" By asking these kinds of questions, you get your mind to focus on what you want to have, do, or be. Then, your mind takes over and answers the question...solves the problem...and creates what you want. You just have to provide the focus, take whatever action presents itself, and be persistent (some things take time).

I would do away with questions like "What's wrong with me?" or "Why can't I find someone to love me?" and so on. Your mind will find an answer to any question you give it, including these disempowering questions.

Learn to say "How can I...?" when you don't know what to do, instead of "I can't," and (if you are persistent in asking) you will receive the answer, every time. Learn to be conscious in what you focus on and your whole life will change.

This all may seem very utopian to you, or overly simplistic, or like a lot of work. I assure you it is not utopian (it's the way all successful people think), it IS simple, but not simplistic, and yes, it is work, at first. The great Napoleon Hill, who spent over 60 years studying the most effective and most successful people of the 20th century, concluded that -- without exception -- "whatever the mind can conceive and believe, it can achieve." He at first suspected there had to be exceptions, but toward the end of his life he said he had to admit he had not found ANY.

Let's go over that again: "Whatever the mind can conceive and believe it can achieve."

It will take some time to learn how to consciously focus your mind. It will require some effort. You will fail many times, and it will seem difficult. But at a certain point you will "get it" and at that point it will become as automatic as the unconscious focusing you have been doing. When that happens, a whole new universe of power will open to you.

More on Focusing

"And be not conformed to this age, but be transformed by the renewing of your mind, in order to prove by you what is the good and pleasing and perfect will of God."

The one thing in your life you can command is your own mind. Whatever negative people and situations you face, you can always choose a positive attitude. But doing so requires a firm, strong commitment.

Helpful: Begin by writing a self-convincing creed – I believe I can direct and control my emotions, intellect and habits with the intention of developing a positive mental attitude. Post it where you'll see it when you get up in the morning. Read it during the day, and say it aloud. Speaking an intention reinforces it. Choose a "self-motivator" – a meaningful phrase tailored to help you reach your positive thinking goals. Examples:

- Counter discouragement with the phrase "Every problem contains the seed of its own solution."

- Fight procrastination with "Do it now."

Keep your self-motivators nearby – in your pocket or on your desk – and repeat them throughout the day to instill these important new values.

Develop A Life Plan. Setting short and long-term goals each day creates a road map for your life. But only set GOOD goals!!! What is a good goal? One where you are 100% in control and one that is founded in love! A goal of raising good, healthy and prosperous children is a bad goal because you are not in control of what your kids choose. See the important difference? The goal is noble but it is not a good goal.

You identify where you're going, focus your mind on getting there and avoid many wrong turns.

Helpful: Use the D-E-S-I-R-E formula as a goal-setting guideline...

- **D**etermine what you want. Be exact, and express the goal positively. Say what you want to be or do rather than what you don't want.

- **E**valuate what you'll give in return. How much work will you do to turn your plan into action?

- **S**et a date for your goal. Be realistic, allowing enough time without postponing it too long.

- **I**dentify a step by step plan. Devise immediate, small steps to get started.

- **R**epeat your plan in writing.

- **E**ach and every day, morning and evening, read your plan aloud as you picture yourself already having achieved your goals.

Writing out your daily goals helps maintain your motivation. Keep them in your pocket or purse to read frequently throughout the day.

The Power of Visualization

Because visual images reach into our deepest mental levels, I have found pictures to be profound motivational tools. Why? Remember the mind holds everything as pictures!

Helpful: Make a list of personal qualities you want to develop...write down the names of people with whom you would like to have better relationships. Now clip pictures from magazines and newspapers that symbolize your goals.

Example: If generosity is your chosen quality, you could use a photo of someone with an outstretched hand.

Put the pictures where you'll see them everyday...and believe that you will get what you have visualized. You may also create your own "mental pictures" to defeat negative thoughts, such as dwelling on past reversals. Maintain A Positive Focus. Giving yourself positive experiences actually reinforces your positive attitude. Examples...

- Treat your five senses every day. Listen to your favorite music, taste a food you love, enjoy a beautiful view, etc.

- Cultivate a sense of humor. Laughter relaxes tension, and seeing the funny side of things helps you take yourself less seriously.

- Smile when you feel like frowning. Smile at yourself in the mirror. If this makes you laugh at yourself, the smile will be that much more real.

Now realize the optimistic face you show the world creates positive thoughts about you in everyone you meet.

How to Train Your Subconscious Mind
Did you know that often the difference between success and failure is the ability to train your mind to focus on achieving your goals and not focus on problems? It's been proven by researchers and by some of the most successful people in the world.

Getting your mind to focus and concentrate on success - so that it finds solutions instead of focusing on the problems is usually the difference between success and failure. But how do you do this?

I'm about to show you how. I'll outline the importance of training your mind, how to start directing your subconscious mind, and how to keep your mind focused so that you constantly achieve your goals and live the life you want. Disciplining your mind so that it is focused on your goals is crucial to your success. If your mind is not trained to focus on and achieve your goals then you really have little chance of success. Your conscious mind is a direct link to your subconscious mind.

So if your mind is focused on your goals and is trained to achieve those goals then your subconscious mind will also be focused on those goals and will attract the situations and opportunities for you to achieve the success you want. It's really that simple.

The minute you get distracted for a prolonged period - you lose sight of your objective and fail to accomplish those goals. In order for to enjoy success - the mind has to be regularly focused on your goals - you can't stay focused for short bursts and expect to get results.

Think of it this way, your riding in a car driven by your personal driver and every time your driver asks you where you want to go you simply say: "I don't know. Wherever you want to go is fine with me." Then when your driver takes you to the place of his choice you complain and say: "I don't want to be here, take me somewhere else." And again you say you don't know where you want to go.

Can you see the confusion you would create? Can you see how you would never get to where you want to go because you haven't trained your driver to automatically take you where you want to go? You haven't given him the proper instructions.

Your mind and subconscious mind work the same way. If you don't train your mind to focus on your goals then your subconscious mind cannot create the situations that will help you achieve those goals. When you keep changing your mind, when you are not clear on what you want - your subconscious gets confused - and you end up exactly where you don't want to be.

Let's go back to the example of your personal driver. Wouldn't it be a lot easier and more comfortable if you told your driver where you wanted to go - or even better - your driver knew where you wanted to go ahead of time? But that will only happen when you train your driver by repeatedly telling him where you want to go on a regular basis.

Your subconscious mind is your driver. Your subconscious gets its instructions from your thoughts and beliefs. Give your subconscious the right instructions and it will take you where ever you want to go in life. When your mind is focused on your goals you direct your subconscious to create opportunities for you to achieve your goals. Your responsibility is to follow up on these opportunities.

How You Can Train Your Mind
Believe it or not I get a lot of calls and emails everyday from people who want to achieve their goals but simply can't get their mind to focus on the tasks that need to be done to have the success that they want. This happens

because the mind is simply not used to focusing on your goals and following up with completing those tasks. So how do you get your mind to change? How do you train your mind?

The first step is to get the mind to stop doing what it is used to doing - or break the pattern that you've been following for so long. This will require some effort - but the reward will allow you to live the life you want and enjoy the level of success that you want.

To re-train your mind and direct your subconscious mind you start by paying more attention - so that when you see yourself getting distracted and not following up on things that you wanted to do - you take a step to break the pattern. You can break the pattern by doing something else. For example: you can start following up on what you had planned to do, you can create a list and follow up with it regularly to see if you are on track.

One thing that always works is to think about your goals every morning. As you're in bed, think about your goals and think about what you can do to achieve them during the day. If you find that you constantly say: "I don't know what do to do to achieve my goals." Then you're not looking for answers in the right place.

Take a look at what other people have done to achieve similar goals and see if you can follow the same process. For example: If you want to make more money take a look at someone else who has made a lot of money and see what they've done. Can you follow their process? Maybe you can even talk to them about the process? If you want to meet someone and be in a healthy relationship, talk to a friend who is in a successful relationship and find out what they did. By doing the above exercises you train your mind to focus on finding solutions while at the same time you direct your subconscious mind to create the opportunities for you to succeed. And - you begin to create a new pattern of thinking and you start to train the mind to work differently. You're now telling your driver where you want to go. This eliminates the confusion and allows you to achieve your goals.

You're not going to magically get your mind to focus or concentrate without you taking some form of action. When you finally do take some action your mind will still resist - but as you continue taking action the resistance will subside - REPITITION. So what action can you take? First start with the exercise I just outlined above. Next - meditate. Meditation is one of the best ways to relax and calm your mind while training it to focus on what you want. When you meditate you actually start to clear the clutter that dominates your mind.

Make the Time
Finally it seems a lot of people have come to believe that they just don't have the time to achieve their goals. If you are one of the many who have such a belief then you've really convinced yourself that your goals are not worthy of your time; because if they were you would make the time for them. I'm not talking about spending an entire day or even a few hours. It's only a few minutes at different intervals. Why try to get everything crammed into one hour? Why not try to think about your goals at different intervals during the day? For example: you may have a few minutes while you're taking a walk - think of your achieving your goals. You could also do this while you're taking a shower, driving, walking, anytime. Here's a suggestion; the next time you are driving or taking a

shower, pay attention to your thoughts. Are these thoughts actually working for your or against you? Would it be better to focus on your goals or keep recycling the negative clutter or junk in your head? The choice is yours - and taking action is really about taking a small step. You don't need to spend hours meditating. Even if you simply mediated for 5 or 10 minutes a day you'd be able to increase your ability to concentrate and focus by a 100-percent within a matter of days! Do it for weeks or months and you'll have dramatic results!

How to Put Your Mind to Sleep Quickly and Rest Completely

If you often lay awake, unable to put your mind to rest while you're tossing and turning, you're going to love what you're about to read, because I'm about to share with you one of the most powerful methods for quickly shutting off your mind, and drifting off to sleep.

As you may already know, your mind must be in the Alpha brain-wave stage to fall asleep. This is the stage your mind enters you're still conscious, but your body and begin to relax. It enables your more rampant and conscious mind to turn off as you enter the realm of sleep. We all know how it feels... when you're lying awake in bed trying to fall asleep, it seems like your mind is running on hyper-speed. It's almost like you're thinking 10 times faster than when you're just normally awake and alert. In fact, if you experience this often, I can tell you for a fact that your mind IS working harder than it is when you're not trying to fall asleep, and there is a very good reason for it, here's why this happens. In my books and articles on sleep, I often teach a principle: "What you focus on expands." You see, your mind responds to focus, and it goes hand in hand with the law of momentum. What is the law of momentum? Quite simply:

"Energy in motion, tends to STAY in motion"

"Energy stopped, tends to STAY stopped"

In other words, if you take action in your life, and begin to create success, you will experience more and more success every day. Success breeds success. On the other hand, if you sit your butt down on the couch to watch TV and say, "Aww, just one show, I'll only watch one show," very soon you'll be sitting there for four hours, and you'll watch five or six shows.

The law of momentum is everywhere in life, in physics, with your body, and most importantly, with your "thoughts." You see, your thinking is very predictable; it all works on the law of focus and momentum. Your mind is like a big ball of potential thinking energy, just waiting for you to give it a direction to think wildly into. It awaits and responds your every command. It's an exceptional tool except, most of us aren't very experienced at "controlling" this amazing tool. In fact, a lot people aren't even aware that they can control it! And this is where sleep problems come in.

Imagine your mind like a giant overflowing lake that's just waiting for an outlet to pour into... Slowly, when it finds an outlet, it begins with a trickle of water. That trickle turns into a stream. Then, that stream turns into a small river. Pretty soon, the small river is a giant unstoppable waterfall. Your thoughts work in the same way when you're "trying" to fall asleep.

For example, you're lying in bed, frustrated, forcing your mind to not think. "I just want to get some sleep! Stop thinking! Okay, starting now... I won't think anymore. No think... nothing. My life is nothing... If only I would finally get motivated in my job maybe I would finally create the income to start traveling instead of dealing with these problems. Problems, how can I... Ahh, I'm thinking again! Stop it!"

You get even more frustrated, and repeat the process over again in a few minutes. So how do you stop it? It's easy, you see, you can easily control your thinking, except most people aren't aware of the tools necessary! The good news is, I'm about to give you the 3-step handbook to controlling your mind. Here are the 3-universal steps that will enable you to not only stop thinking; you'll also be able to lower your brain-waves into the alpha brain-state, which will quickly let you enter sleep...

Awareness

The first step to changing anything is becoming aware that it's happening, especially if it's your mind. Pretend your mind is racing, and you finally realize that you're thinking... Most people at this stage get extremely frustrated and "try" to force the mind into submission. It doesn't work! Why? Because, what you focus on expands. The more frustrated you get, the more you're focusing on frustration, so you'll get even MORE frustration and more thinking... on and on!

So the first step is to simply become "aware" of the fact that you're thinking. Nothing more. When you notice that you're thinking, smile to yourself, and say, "I just noticed myself thinking... Interesting..." Now notice what happens inside of you when you do this... something

VERY profound. If "I" just noticed "myself" thinking, perhaps there are really two completely separate identities running your life? There is the "I" and there is the "self."

The "I", is the real you, the higher being, the "I" behind the mind, that runs the show, the heart, the soul, the true conscious being, the choice maker.

The "self" is the mind; if left to run the show, it will run in endless circles until the edge of insanity.

The moment you do this, the moment you become "aware" - you are no longer a slave to your mind. You have won. After you become aware... do nothing, just lay there for 3 seconds and notice how it feels to be present in who you really are, not the mind, but you, the "I" - there is a great feeling of peace behind that presence in the "I." Why? Because when you are aware like this, you're aware of the power of your choice making. You now have the power of choice.

Relaxed Focus
"What you focus on expands." Now that you have become aware of your thinking, all you have to do is "direct" your mind into a place that will bring you into a deep, deep place of relaxation. Think about it, if before your mind will relentlessly race into any direction you give it; why not pick a direction that will give you peace and restful sleep?

But, most people don't know what that direction really is. It's really easy. If you focus on anything your body does or feels subconsciously, you will begin to become more and more realized. For example your breathing, the feeling of the pillow on your head, the sounds of nature outside (unless you live in the city), the warmth of your body. These are all things that happen, yet your conscious mind doesn't think about them.

As you know, "What you focus on expands"... So what would happen if you focused on something that is happening in your "subconscious"? That's right, your conscious thinking would diminish, and your subconscious mind would begin to take over the entire process of you falling asleep! It really is that simple, and it works every-time.

The easiest one is your breathing. And I promise you if you just try this tonight, you will be shocked when you wake up in the morning: "Wow! It worked!"

Repetition
As I said, the easiest one to focus on is your breathing. In the beginning, you'll find this easier said than done. Let me walk you through it.

- Begin by taking your focus onto your breathing. Take a deep breath in. Hold it for a short while, and slowly exhale...

- Count "1"

- Breathe in again... hold it shortly, exhale slowly, and count...

- "2"

Why count? Because I guarantee you, in the very beginning, you may find it challenging to hold your focus. In fact, you'll be surprised as you may not even make it to "5" the first time. This is because your conscious ever-thinking mind will butt in and interrupt. You may randomly go off into a barrage of thoughts again. If this happens, and it very well may, what do you do?

Simply become aware, and begin focusing on your breathing again. Guess what happens? As you become aware, 2 or 3 times... your mind will give up. I guarantee you, beyond the shadow of a doubt, when you get to "10" or "15" breaths you will feel a wave of relaxation in your body. This is the silent "click" as your mind shifts from the high frequency Beta brain-waves into Alpha brain-waves. Your subconscious mind will do the rest!

The following exercise will teach you how to see and recognize things that are unworthy of attention, but still recognize that they are there. In other words, attention will be paid to it and then discarded. A filter makes you totally oblivious (no attention given to it at all) that the stimuli are there and if asked to describe the situation, the filter will cause you to omit it.

Chapter 2 – Perception Investing

In Chapter 1, I provided you with a small introduction into behavioral science. My goal was for you to better understand why you and others do the things you do.

The mechanism of the mind is used in all cases to determine a person's action or reactions to everything around them and to those things that come into a person through their 5-senses.

It is especially important to understand the difference between the conscious mind and the subconscious mind. All behavior stems from the subconscious mind so all emotional responses to whatever occurs in the marketplace comes from a person's subconscious mind.

It is also important to note that there are significant gender differences in behavioral science and the female investor is quite different from the male investor.

But most important of all is realizing that the conscious mind "sees" reality for what it is but the subconscious mind "perceives" that same reality and the perception can be quite different than the reality itself.

Perception investing is looking at the factual or real market indicators and then comparing these to the emotional factors or the "subconscious' mind perception" or understanding of the real market indicators.

Let me give you an example....

Many of my readers weren't around back in 1987 when Black Monday occurred. Either you were too young or you weren't even born yet but I know some of you remember the market crash on October 19, 1987.

Here is a brief description of it I took from Wikipedia:

In finance, **Black Monday** refers to Monday October 19, 1987, when stock markets around the world crashed, shedding a huge value in a very short time. The crash began in Hong Kong and spread west to Europe, hitting the United States after other markets had already declined by a significant margin. The Dow Jones Industrial

Average (DJIA) dropped by 508 points to 1738.74 (22.61%).

Potential causes for the decline include program trading, overvaluation, illiquidity, and **market psychology.**

The most popular explanation for the 1987 crash was selling by program traders. U.S. Congressman Edward J. Markey, who had been warning about the possibility of a crash, stated that "Program trading was the principal cause." In program trading, computers perform rapid stock executions based on external inputs, such as the price of related securities. Common strategies implemented by program trading involve an attempt to engage in arbitrage and *portfolio insurance* strategies. The trader Paul Tudor Jones predicted and profited from the crash, attributing it to portfolio insurance strategies which were "an accident waiting to happen" and that the "crash was something that was eminently forecastable". Once the market started going down, portfolio insurance futures sellers were "forced to sell on every down-tick" so the "selling would actually cascade instead of dry up".

As computer technology became more available, the use of program trading grew dramatically within Wall Street firms. After the crash, many blamed program trading strategies for blindly selling stocks as markets fell, exacerbating the decline. Some economists theorized the speculative boom leading up to October was caused by program trading, and that the crash was merely a return to normalcy. Either way, program trading ended up taking the majority of the blame in the public eye for the 1987 stock market crash.

New York University's Richard Sylla divides the causes into macroeconomic and internal reasons. Macroeconomic causes included international disputes about foreign exchange and interest rates, and fears about inflation.

The internal reasons included innovations with index futures and portfolio insurance. I've seen accounts that maybe roughly half the trading on that day was a small number of institutions with portfolio insurance. Big guys were dumping their stock. Also, the futures market in Chicago was even lower than the stock market, and people tried to arbitrage that. The proper strategy was to buy futures in Chicago and sell in the New York cash market. It made it hard -- the portfolio insurance people were also trying to sell their stock at the same time.

Economist Richard Roll believes the international nature of the stock market decline contradicts the argument that program trading was to blame. Program trading strategies were used primarily in the United States, Roll writes. Markets where program trading was not prevalent, such as Australia and Hong Kong, would not have declined as well, if program trading was the cause. These markets might have been reacting to excessive program trading in the United States, but Roll indicates otherwise. The crash began on October 19 in Hong Kong, spread west to Europe, and hit the United States only after Hong Kong and other markets had already declined by a significant margin.

Another common theory states that the crash was a result of a dispute in monetary policy between the G7 industrialized nations, in which the United States, wanting to prop up the dollar and restrict inflation, tightened policy faster than the Europeans. U.S. pressure on Germany to change its monetary policy was one of the factors that unnerved investors in the run-up to the crash. The crash, in this view, was caused when the dollar-backed Hong Kong stock exchange collapsed, and this caused a crisis in confidence.

Some technical analysts claim that the cause was the collapse of the US and European bond markets, which caused interest-sensitive stock groups like savings & loans and money center banks to plunge as well. This is a well documented inter-market relationship: turns in bond markets affect interest-rate-sensitive stocks, which in turn lead the general stock market turns.

*****

One of the key points of the article above is the statement, "Potential causes for the decline include program trading, overvaluation, illiquidity, and **market psychology.**" I placed the bold emphasis on the words "market psychology".

Most finance people will acknowledge in private that "Bias, Emotion, & Overconfidence" does drive the market in a significant way; however in public, these factors are often ignored or listed last in any analysis like the Wikipedia article.

If you are wondering why, the only thing I can attribute this to is that finance people in general like to be "in control" and when dealing with the emotional factors that drive the market, they ARE NOT in control nor do they even have the ability to analyze the emotional market factors.

Okay, back to my example...

As the article above states, Black Monday occurred on October 19, 1987. On Friday October 16, 1987 I was in my investment banker's office in Ottawa, Canada along with my CFO.

In the course of my meeting I order my investment banker to buy $3 million in IBJ (Industrial Bank of Japan) Eurobonds.

Bonds are also known as debentures or debt instruments and are different than stocks, which are also called "equities". The price of a bond is indirectly proportional to the interest rate of a bond. In other words, when the price of the bond rises, the interest rate declines and when the price of the bond declines the interest rate rises.

My investment banker left the conference room to place the order and when he had left, my CFO leaned over and whispered to me, "I do not have $3 million in liquidity to pay for this order." I just patted his hand and told him not to worry about it but it was his Job to WORRY about it and I will tell you why in just a moment...

In high finance, when you are playing with the big boys, everything is done based on your word. My investment banker soon returned and put me on the speaker phone with the trader at the desk in London for Prudential Securities (at the time all Eurobonds traded through London at Prudential Securities) to confirm the order.

The trader spoke, "Sir, I have an order for $3 million in IBJ at x-price for immediate delivery to DTC in New York. Do you confirm this order, sir?"

My response, "Yes, the order is confirmed."

The minute I confirmed the order I owned $3 million in IBJ and my CFO cringed I might add.

What happened next was the trader assigned CUSIP numbers to $3 million in IBJ bonds, thus activating them and sent them to DTC (Depository Trust Company) in New York which acted as the clearinghouse. A clearing house is like an escrow service in real estate. It receives the activated bonds and verifies the CUSIP numbers then exchanges the bonds for the $3 million in cash in my account. It sends the $3-million to Prudential Securities and then places the bonds in my account in DTC, which is a subaccount to my bank at the time – Bankers Trust.

For those of you that do not know what a CUSIP number is - a CUSIP is a 9-character alphanumeric code which identifies a North American financial security for the purposes of facilitating clearing and settlement of trades.

The acronym *CUSIP* derives from the Committee on Uniform Security Identification Procedures, which was founded in 1964 and developed the CUSIP system. In the 1980s there was an attempt to expand the CUSIP code system for international securities as well.

Okay all this occurred on Friday, October 16, 1987 and as you know the crash came Monday morning on October 19, 1987. In other words, before my IBJ bonds could be delivered, they had increased in value by 3% or $90,000. Of course none of this was known on the Friday in the conference room and I knew when my CFO and I left that he would be on the computer looking to find $3 million in assets that he could liquidate to pay for the order.

Since everything is based on your word, woe it will be to the person that confirmed the order if $3 million is not in DTC when those bonds are delivered because I would be "black balled' from ever buying Eurobonds again and my CFO knew this so he immediately went to work to make sure there was $3 million in the DTC account.

Now, just to be clear; I just look stupid. At the time, sitting in my Bankers Trust account was over $50 million in "paid-for" Eurobonds that my CFO could easily leverage or margin to pay for the order but my CFO was the type of accountant that did not believe in debt and the word "margin" was a dirty word. He would use my portfolio only as a last resort. To him it was easier to liquidate CDs (certificates of deposits) and things of this nature with small penalties.

Anyway, his efforts were futile because the market crashed before the bonds were delivered and I flipped my whole Eurobond portfolio ($53 million) on that Monday morning earning $1,590,000.

So what happened in layman terms? Remember above how I described bonds..."Bonds are also known as debentures or debt instruments and are different than stocks, which are also called "equities". The price of a bond is indirectly proportional to the interest rate of a bond. In other words, when the price of the bond rises, the interest rate of the bond declines and when the price of the bond declines the interest rate rises.

What happened on Black Monday was that all debentures prices declined significantly beginning in Hong Kong and then moving west into Europe and then the United States. As the prices on debentures declined the interest rate went up. So I ended up making over 1.5 million dollars on a portfolio of $53 million in Eurobond debentures because the decline increased the interest rate by 3-points.

Now a 3-point move is enormous. Usually bonds move in increments of $1/16^{th}$ of a point or what is known in the industry as a "steenth". The crash of the market caused the 3-point increase in interest and made the bonds very favorable for selling.

The crash caused my CFO another headache. He was now sitting on a horde of cash from my selling off the entire portfolio that he needed to "get working' so he and his staff were very busy that Monday.

After it was all said and done and the "dust had settled' my CFO came and sat in my office and wanted to know how I knew the market was going to crash. Even my investment banker had called and asked the same thing. The short answer, I didn't know it was going to crash that Monday and I knew that my CFO would find the liquidity to pay for the $3 million order. What I did know was that the market would crash. It wasn't a matter of 'if" but only and matter of "when".

At the time, the market was so inflated with no rational reason for it being so high that even an amateur could see the writing on the wall. What did take me by surprise was that it began in Hong Kong. The Asian mind is quite different than the Caucasian mind but that is another book.

What occurred on Monday, October 19, 1987 is nothing new and if fact it is something that is quite old. The following is a list of stock market crashes taken from Wikipedia that I think you will find most interesting…

List of Stock Market Crashes

http://en.wikipedia.org/wiki/List_of_stock_market_crashes_and_bear_markets

Name	Dates	Country	Causes	Ref

Name	Dates	Country	Causes	Ref
Kipper und Wipper	1623		Financial crisis during the start of the Thirty Years' War (1621-1623)	[1]
Tulip mania Bubble	1637		A bubble (1633-37) in Netherlands during which contracts for bulbs of tulips reached extraordinarily high prices, and suddenly collapsed	[2]
The Mississippi Bubble	1720		Banque Royale by John Law stopped payments of its note in exchange for specie and as result caused economic collapse in France.	
South Sea	1720		Affected early	

Name	Dates	Country	Causes	Ref
Bubble of 1720			European stock markets, during early days of chartered joint stock companies	
Bengal Bubble of 1769	1769	🇬🇧	Primarily caused by the British East India Company, whose shares fell from £276 in December 1768 to £122 in 1784	
Panic of 1796–1797	1796			
Panic of 1819	1819			
Panic of 1837	10 May 1837			
Panic of 1847	1847			
Panic of 1857	1857			
Black Friday	24 Sep 1869			

Name	Dates	Country	Causes	Ref
Panic of 1873	9 May 1873		Initiated the Long Depression in the United States and much of Europe	
Paris Bourse crash of 1882	19 Jan 1882			
Panic of 1884	1884			
Encilhamento	1886		Lasting 3 years, 1890-1893, a Boom and bust process that *boomed* in late 1880s and *burst* on early 1890s, causing a collapse in the Brazilian economy and aggravating an already unstable political situation.	[3][4][5][6]
Panic of	1893			

Name	Dates	Country	Causes	Ref
1893				
Panic of 1896	1896			
Panic of 1901	17 May 1901	🇺🇸	Lasting 3 years, the market was spooked by the assassination of President McKinley in 1901, coupled with a severe drought later the same year.	
Panic of 1907	Oct 1907	🇺🇸	Lasting over a year, markets took fright after U.S. President Theodore Roosevelt had threatened to rein in the monopolies that flourished in various industrial sectors, notably	

Name	Dates	Country	Causes	Ref
Wall Street Crash of 1929	24 Oct 1929		railways. Lasting over 4 years, the bursting of the speculative bubble in shares led to further selling as people who had borrowed money to buy shares had to cash them in, when their loans were called in. Also called the Great Crash or the Wall Street Crash, leading to the Great Depression.	
Recession of 1937–1938 (U.S.)	1937		Lasting around a year, this share price fall was triggered by an economic	

67

Name	Dates	Country	Causes	Ref
			recession within the Great Depression and doubts about the effectiveness of Franklin D. Roosevelt's New Deal policy.	
1971 Brazilian Markets Crash	July 1971		Lasting through the 1970s and early-1980s, this was the end of a boom starting in 1969, compounded by the 1970s energy crisis coupled with early 1980s Latin American debt crisis.	[7][8][9]
1973–1974 stock market crash	Jan 1973		Lasting 23 months, dramatic rise	

Name	Dates	Country	Causes	Ref
			in oil prices, the miners' strike and the downfall of the Heath government.	
Silver Thursday	27 March 1980		Silver price crash	
Souk Al-Manakh stock market crash	Aug 1982			
Black Monday	**19 Oct 1987**			
Rio de Janeiro Stock Exchange collapse	June 1989		Rio Stock Exchange Crash, due its weak internal controls and absence of credit discipline, that led to its collapse, and of which it never recovered	[10][11][12]
Friday the 13th mini-crash	13 Oct 1989		Failed leveraged buyout of	

Name	Dates	Country	Causes	Ref
			United Airlines causes crash	
Japanese asset price bubble	1991		Lasting 13 years, until 2003, share and property price bubble bursts and turns into a long deflationary recession.	
Black Wednesday	16 Sep 1992		The Conservative government was forced to withdraw the pound sterling from the European Exchange Rate Mechanism (ERM) after they were unable to keep sterling above its agreed lower	

Name	Dates	Country	Causes	Ref
1997 Asian financial crisis	2 July 1997		limit. Investors deserted emerging Asian shares, including an overheated Hong Kong stock market. Crashes occur in Thailand, Indonesia, South Korea, Philippines, and elsewhere, reaching a climax in the October 27, 1997 mini-crash.	
October 27, 1997 mini-crash	27 Oct 1997		Global stock market crash that was caused by an economic crisis in Asia. The points loss that the Dow Jones	

Name	Dates	Country	Causes	Ref
			Industrial Average suffered on this day still ranks as the seventh biggest point loss in its 114-year existence.	
1998 Russian financial crisis	17 Aug 1998		The Russian government devalues the ruble, defaults on domestic debt, and declares a moratorium on payment to foreign creditors.	
Dot-com bubble	10 March 2000	3 years	Collapse of a technology bubble, world economic effects arising from the September 11 attacks and the stock	

Name	Dates	Country	Causes	Ref
Economic effects arising from the September 11 attacks	11 Sep 2001		market downturn of 2002. The September 11 attacks caused global stock markets to drop sharply. The attacks themselves caused approximately $40 billion in insurance losses, making it one of the largest insured events ever.	
Stock market downturn of 2002	9 Oct 2002		Downturn in stock prices during 2002 in stock exchanges across the United States, Canada, Asia, and Europe. After	

Name	Dates	Country	Causes	Ref
			recovering from lows reached following the September 11 attacks, indices slid steadily starting in March 2002, with dramatic declines in July and September leading to lows last reached in 1997 and 1998.	
Chinese stock bubble of 2007	27 Feb 2007		The SSE Composite Index of the Shanghai Stock Exchange tumbles 9% from unexpected selloffs, the largest drop in 10 years,	[13][14][15]

Name	Dates	Country	Causes	Ref
			triggering major drops in worldwide stock markets.	
United States bear market of 2007–2009	11 Oct 2007		Till June 2009, the Dow Jones Industrial Average, Nasdaq Composite and S&P 500 all experienced declines of greater than 20% from their peaks in late 2007.	[16][17]
Late-2000s financial crisis	16 Sep 2008		On September 16, 2008, failures of large financial institutions in the United States, due primarily to exposure of securities of packaged	[18][19]

Name	Dates	Country	Causes	Ref
			subprime loans and credit default swaps issued to insure these loans and their issuers, rapidly devolved into a global crisis resulting in a number of bank failures in Europe and sharp reductions in the value of equities (stock) and commodities worldwide. The failure of banks in Iceland resulted in a devaluation of the Icelandic króna and threatened the government with	

Name	Dates	Country	Causes	Ref
			bankruptcy. Iceland was able to secure an emergency loan from the IMF in November. Later on, U.S. President George W. Bush signs the Emergency Economic Stabilization Act into law, creating a Troubled Asset Relief Program (TARP) to purchase failing bank assets.	
2009 Dubai debt standstill	November 27, 2009		Dubai requests a debt deferment following its massive renovation	[20]

Name	Dates	Country	Causes	Ref
European sovereign debt crisis	27 April 2010		and development projects, as well as the late-2000s recession. The announcement causes global stock markets to drop. Standard & Poor's downgrades Greece's sovereign credit rating to junk four days after the activation of a €45-billion EU–IMF bailout, triggering the decline of stock markets worldwide and of the Euro's value, and furthering a European	[21][22][23]

Name	Dates	Country	Causes	Ref
2010 Flash Crash	6 May 2010		sovereign debt crisis. The Dow Jones Industrial Average suffers its worst intra-day point loss, dropping nearly 1,000 points before partially recovering.	[24]
August 2011 stock markets fall	Aug 2011		Stock markets around the world plummet during late July and early August, and are volatile for the rest of the year.	

Okay, now let's move on and discuss what is known as the Noise Trader Theory

Chapter 3 – Noise Trader Theory

Rather than get into an "oral dissertation of what a Noise trader Theory is, allow me to use another Wikipedia article to explain it:

Noise Trader
From Wikipedia, the free encyclopedia
Jump to: navigation, search

A **noise trader** also known informally as **idiot trader**[1] is described in the literature of financial research as a stock trader whose decisions to buy, sell, or hold are irrational and erratic. The presence of noise traders in financial markets can then cause prices and risk levels to diverge from expected levels even if all other traders are rational.[2]

In finance, noise obtained a formal definition in a 1986 paper by Fischer Black: "Noise in the sense of a large number of small events is often a cause factor much more powerful than a small number of large events can be."[3]

Notes

1. ^ Krugman, Paul (2009-09-06). "How Did Economists Get It So Wrong?" *The New York Times*. Retrieved 2010-05-20.
2. ^ DeLong, Bradford J.; Shleifer, Andrei; Summers, Larry; Waldmann, Robert J. (1990). "Noise Trader Risk in Financial Markets". *The Journal of Political Economy* (The University of Chicago Press) **98** (4): 703–738. doi:10.1086/261703. JSTOR 2937765.
3. ^ Black, Fischer (1985-12-20). "Noise". *Journal of Finance* **41** (3): 529–543. doi:10.2307/2328481. JSTOR 2328481.

Types of stocks	• Common stock • Golden share • Preferred stock • Restricted stock • Tracking stock
Share capital	• Authorized capital • Issued shares • Shares outstanding • Treasury stock
Participants	• Broker-dealer

	- Floor broker - Floor trader - Investor - Market maker - Proprietary trader - Quantitative analyst - Stock trader
Exchanges	- Electronic communication network - Stock exchange opening times - Over-the-counter - List of stock exchanges - Multilateral trading facility
Stock valuation	- Alpha - Arbitrage pricing theory - Beta - Book value - Capital asset pricing model - Dividend yield - Earnings per share - Earnings yield - Dividend discount model - Security characteristic line - Security market line - T-Model
Trading theories and strategies	- Algorithmic trading - Buy and hold - Concentrated stock - Contrarian investing - Day trading

	- Efficient-market hypothesis - Fundamental analysis - Growth stock - Market timing - Modern portfolio theory - Momentum investing - Mosaic theory - Pairs trade - Post-modern portfolio theory - Random walk hypothesis - Style investing - Swing trading - Technical analysis - Trend following
Related terms	- Block trade - Cross listing - Dark liquidity - Dividend - Dual-listed company - DuPont analysis - Flight-to-quality - Haircut - Initial public offering - Margin - Market anomaly - Market capitalization - Market depth - Market manipulation - Market trend - Mean reversion - Momentum - Open outcry

- Public float
- Public offering
- Rally
- Reverse stock split
- Returns-based style analysis
- Short selling
- Slippage
- Speculation
- Stock dilution
- Stock split
- Trade
- Uptick rule
- Volatility
- Voting interest
- Stock market index

Here is another great but longggggggggg article on the subject:

http://www.jstor.org/discover/10.2307/2328324?uid=3739928&uid=2129&uid=2&uid=70&uid=4&uid=3739256&sid=21102178105267

Definition of 'Noise Trader'

The term used to describe an investor who makes decisions regarding buy and sell trades without the use of fundamental data. These investors generally have poor timing, follow trends, and over-react to good and bad news. A hotly debated issue in behavioral finance, many investors feel that they're not noise traders and, therefore, only make well informed investment decisions. In reality, most people are considered to be noise traders, as very few actually make investment decisions solely using fundamental analysis. Furthermore, technical analysis is considered to be a part of noise trading because the data is unrelated to the fundamentals of a company.

Here is another very good PDF that takes into consideration the Asian mind:

http://www.efmaefm.org/0EFMAMEETINGS/EFMA%20ANNUAL%20MEETINGS/2011-Braga/papers/0248.pdf

Theoretical and Empirical Study on Noise Trading Behavior and Risk of Chinese Stock Market
Posted in Home > Finance & Bank > on 2011-10-14 10:33 | 203 views

http://www.business-finance.org/finance-bank/theoretical-and-empirical-study-on-noise-trading-behavior-and-risk-of-chinese-stock-market.html

With the development of financial market, especially stock market, there emerges a lot of financial abnormal phenomenon which cannot be explained in emerging market economy country which is during market transition period. As an immature emerging market, Chinese stock market is different from mature foreign stock market on background, operation way and development history. There are more noise trade, anormal phenomenon and risk in Chinese stock market. Systematically studying how noise trader impact stock price and the risk from theory and empiric can explain market behavior effectively. So noise trade study has significant meanings of theories and practices to risk management and control, improving governmental regulation effectiveness, guiding investor's investment philosophy and investment decision rightly, even more guarantee Chinese stock market developing healthily, steadily and constantly. The main research work and study conclusion of this paper as follow:

①Using descriptive statistics to analyze Chinese stock investor's behavior characteristics from the sides of the stock investor structure, institutional investor's stock price manipulation behavior, individual investor's trading behavior, short-term buying and selling behavior and so on. The research result shows that the stock investor structure is not reasonable, institutional investor has some stock price manipulation behavior, the individual investor's non-rational trading behavior and short-term buying and selling behavior are a lot. It indicates that there may be a lot of noise trade in Chinese stock market.

②Using econometric model, this paper takes twins stock as empirical example to study the noise trading characteristics in Chinese stock market Based on isolating the noise shocks from the fundamental shocks, the study result indicates that there are both systematic and idiosyncratic noise trade in short-term Chinese stock market. There is more noise trade in short-term Chinese stock market than in long-term market. The systematic noise has noticeable effect to stock price and excess return in long-term Chinese A share market. The volatility caused by the idiosyncratic noise in the market has noticeable time-varying. The idiosyncratic noise risk was smooth between Aug. 2001 and Aug. 2006. It rose sharply between Sep. 2006 and Oct. 2007, and then it declined sharply between Nov. 2007 and Aug. 2008. This study result is identical to reality between Aug. 2001 and Aug. 2008.

③Relaxing the condition that risk asset dividend is constant and changing of stock dividend follow Gaussian distributions in DSSW model, this paper builds a reasonable mathematical model to study how Chinese noise trader influences prices of risky assets and the market risk. Base on it, the author explains the reason why the financial abnormal phenomenon and the high financial risk appear in Chinese stock market. The study result indicates that if there is only rational investor in stock market, stock price is set by true value and volatility of true value. If there are both rational investor and noise trader in the market, stock price may deviate from true value, and the volatility of stock price increases because noise trader may influence stock price. The so-called financial abnormal phenomenon which performs stock large price movement between Jun. 2005 and Aug. 2008 mainly because the noise trader who dominated Chinese stock market became over optimism when stock price rose, whereas became over pessimistic when stock price declined. The conclusion of this paper shows that there are some effective ways of lessening negative impact of noise trader, guaranteeing healthy, steady, constant development of Chinese stock market, like breeding rational investor rapidly, enhancing information transparency, reducing cost of information, instituting and improving related regulation, especially the credit trading system, strengthening financial derivatives developed and popularized, completing government regulation and so on.

LOADING... Tags: Noise trade, Chinese stock market, Twins stock, DSSW model,

Related Posts

- An Empirical Study of Funds' Herding and Its Impact on Stock Prices
- Research of Pricing Options Embedded in Deposits and Loans Using Monte Carlo Simulation
- Fuzzy Clustering Evaluation Algorithm Based on Decision Tree and Application in Securities Business
- Empirical Research for European Option Pricing Models on Levy Processes
- The Optimal Control of Guarantees
- A Parabolic Obstacle Problem Related to Executive Stock Options
- The New CAPM Model Based on Prospect Theory
- The Statistic Research on the Underpricing in IPO under the Verification System
- The Stock Index Time Series Analysis Based on Hybrid Genetic Algorithm
- Study on Mechanism and Process of Venture Capital

I think you get the point, Noise traders make up the bulk of the market, hence they cause quite of bit of emotional or "irrational" trading. Now let's discuss what is called "Efficient Market Hypothesis – EMH".

Chapter 4 - Efficient Market Hypothesis (EMH)

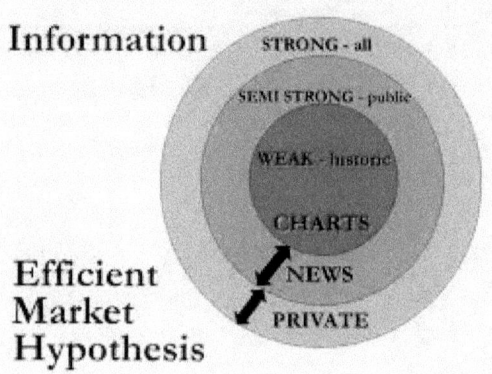

Here is a theory that will really aggravate the snot outta you...

EMH is an investment theory that states it is impossible to "beat the market" because stock market efficiency causes existing share prices to always incorporate and reflect all relevant information. According to the EMH, stocks always trade at their fair value on stock exchanges, making it impossible for investors to either purchase undervalued stocks or sell stocks for inflated prices. As such, it should be impossible to outperform the overall market through expert stock selection or market timing, and that the only way an investor can possibly obtain higher returns is by purchasing riskier investments.

Although it is a cornerstone of modern financial theory, the EMH is highly controversial and often disputed. Believers argue it is pointless to search for undervalued stocks or to try to predict trends in the market through either fundamental or technical analysis.

Meanwhile, while academics point to a large body of evidence in support of EMH, an equal amount of dissension also exists. For example, investors, such as Warren Buffett have consistently beaten the market over long periods of time, which by definition is impossible according to the EMH.

Detractors of the EMH also point to events, such as the 1987 stock market crash when the Dow Jones Industrial Average (DJIA) fell by over 20% in a single day, as evidence that stock prices can seriously deviate from their fair values.

Here is an article from Wikipedia that I find amazing. Read it first then we will discuss it.

Efficient-market hypothesis

http://en.wikipedia.org/wiki/Efficient-market_hypothesis

In finance, the **efficient-market hypothesis** (**EMH**) asserts that financial markets are "informationally efficient". In consequence of this, one cannot consistently achieve returns in excess of average market returns on a risk-adjusted basis, given the information available at the time the investment is made.

There are three major versions of the hypothesis: "weak", "semi-strong", and "strong". The weak-form EMH claims that prices on traded assets (*e.g.,* stocks, bonds, or property) already reflect all past publicly available information. The semi-strong-form EMH claims both that prices reflect all publicly available information and that prices instantly change to reflect new public information. The strong-form EMH additionally claims that prices instantly reflect even hidden or "insider" information. Critics have blamed the belief in rational markets for much of the late-2000s financial crisis. In response, proponents of the hypothesis have stated that market efficiency does not mean having no uncertainty about the future, that market efficiency is a simplification of the world which may not always hold true, and that the market is practically efficient for investment purposes for most individuals.

Historical background

Historically, there was a very close link between EMH and the random-walk model and then the Martingale model. The random character of stock market prices was first modeled by Jules Regnault, a French broker, in 1863 and then by Louis Bachelier, a French mathematician, in his 1900 PhD thesis, "The Theory of Speculation". His work was largely ignored until the 1950s; however beginning in the 1930s scattered, independent work corroborated his thesis. A small number of studies indicated that US stock prices and related financial series followed a random walk model. Research by Alfred Cowles in the '30s and '40s suggested that professional investors were in general unable to outperform the market.

The efficient-market hypothesis was developed by Professor Eugene Fama at the University of Chicago Booth School of Business as an academic concept of study through his published Ph.D. thesis in the early 1960s at the same school. It was widely accepted up until the 1990s, when behavioral finance economists, who had been a fringe element, became mainstream. Empirical analyses have consistently found problems with the efficient-market hypothesis, the most consistent being that stocks with low price to earnings (and similarly, low price to cash-flow or book value) outperform other stocks. Alternative theories have proposed that cognitive biases cause these inefficiencies, leading investors to purchase overpriced growth stocks rather than value stocks. Although the efficient-market hypothesis has become controversial because substantial and lasting inefficiencies are observed, Beechey et al. (2000) consider that it remains a worthwhile starting point.

The efficient-market hypothesis emerged as a prominent theory in the mid-1960s. Paul Samuelson had begun to circulate Bachelier's work among economists. In 1964 Bachelier's dissertation along with the empirical studies mentioned above were published in an anthology edited by Paul Cootner. In 1965 Eugene Fama published his dissertation arguing for the random walk hypothesis, and Samuelson published a proof for a version of the efficient-market hypothesis. In 1970 Fama published a review of both the theory and the evidence for the hypothesis. The paper extended and refined the theory, included the definitions for three forms of financial market efficiency: weak, semi-strong and strong (see below).

It has been argued that the stock market is "micro efficient" but not "macro efficient". The main proponent of this view was Samuelson, who asserted that the EMH is much better suited for individual stocks than it is for the aggregate stock market. Research based on regression and scatter diagrams has strongly supported Samuelson's dictum.

Further to this evidence that the UK stock market is weak-form efficient, other studies of capital markets have pointed toward their being semi-strong-form efficient. A study by Khan of the grain futures market indicated semi-strong form efficiency following the release of large trader position information (Khan, 1986). Studies by Firth (1976, 1979, and 1980) in the United Kingdom have compared the share prices existing after a takeover announcement with the bid offer. Firth found that the share prices were fully and instantaneously adjusted to their correct levels, thus concluding that the UK stock market was semi-strong-form efficient. However, the market's ability to efficiently respond to a short term, widely publicized event such as a takeover announcement does not necessarily prove market efficiency related to other more long term, amorphous factors. David Dreman has criticized the evidence provided by this instant "efficient" response, pointing out that an immediate response is not necessarily efficient, and that the long-term performance of the stock in response to certain movements is better indications.

Theoretical background

Beyond the normal utility maximizing agents, the efficient-market hypothesis requires that agents have rational expectations; that on average the population is correct (even if no one person is) and whenever new relevant information appears, the agents update their expectations appropriately. Note that it is not required that the agents be rational. EMH allows that when faced with new information, some investors may overreact and some may underreact. All that is required by the EMH is that investors' reactions be random and follow a normal distribution pattern so that the net effect on market prices cannot be reliably exploited to make an abnormal profit, especially when considering transaction costs (including commissions and spreads). Thus, any one person can be wrong about the market—indeed, everyone can be—but the market as a whole is always right. There are three common forms in which the efficient-market hypothesis is commonly stated—**weak-form efficiency**, **semi-strong-form efficiency** and **strong-form efficiency**, each of which has different implications for how markets work.

In **weak-form efficiency**, future prices cannot be predicted by analyzing prices from the past. Excess returns cannot be earned *in the long run* by using investment strategies based on historical share prices or other historical data. Technical analysis techniques will not be able to consistently produce excess returns, though some forms of fundamental analysis may still provide excess returns. Share prices exhibit no serial dependencies, meaning that there are no "patterns" to asset prices. This implies that future price movements are determined entirely by information not contained in the price series. Hence, prices must follow a random walk. This 'soft' EMH does not require that prices remain at or near equilibrium, but only that market participants not be able to *systematically* profit from market 'inefficiencies'. However, while EMH predicts that all price movement (in the absence of change in fundamental information) is random (i.e., non-trending), many studies have shown a marked tendency for the stock markets to trend over time periods of weeks or longer and that, moreover, there is a positive correlation between degree of trending and length of time period studied (but note that over long time periods, the trending is sinusoidal in appearance). Various explanations for such large and apparently non-random price movements have been promulgated.

The problem of algorithmically constructing prices which reflect all available information has been studied extensively in the field of computer science. For example, the complexity of finding the arbitrage opportunities in pair betting markets has been shown to be NP-hard.

In **semi-strong-form efficiency**, it is implied that share prices adjust to publicly available new information very rapidly and in an unbiased fashion, such that no excess returns can be earned by trading on that information. Semi-strong-form efficiency implies that neither fundamental analysis nor technical analysis techniques will be able to reliably produce excess returns. To test for semi-strong-form efficiency, the adjustments to previously unknown news must be of a reasonable size and must be instantaneous. To test for this, consistent upward or downward adjustments after the initial change must be looked for. If there are any such adjustments it would suggest that investors had interpreted the information in a biased fashion and hence in an inefficient manner.

In **strong-form efficiency**, share prices reflect all information, public and private, and no one can earn excess returns. If there are legal barriers to private information becoming public, as with insider trading laws, strong-form efficiency is impossible, except in the case where the laws are universally ignored. To test for strong-form efficiency, a market needs to exist where investors cannot consistently earn excess returns over a long period of time. Even if some money managers are consistently observed to beat the market, no refutation even of strong-form efficiency follows: with hundreds of thousands of fund managers worldwide, even a normal distribution of returns (as efficiency predicts) should be expected to produce a few dozen "star" performers.

Criticism and behavioral finance

Price-Earnings ratios as a predictor of twenty-year returns based upon the plot by Robert Shiller (Figure 10.1, source). The horizontal axis shows the real price-earnings ratio of the S&P Composite Stock Price Index as computed in *Irrational Exuberance* (inflation adjusted price divided by the prior ten-year mean of inflation-adjusted earnings). The vertical axis shows the geometric average real annual return on investing in the S&P Composite Stock Price Index, reinvesting dividends, and selling twenty years later. Data from different twenty-year periods is color-coded as shown in the key. See also ten-year returns. Shiller states that this plot "confirms that long-term investors—investors who commit their money to an investment for ten full years—did do well when prices were low relative to earnings at the beginning of the ten years. Long-term investors would be well advised, individually, to lower their exposure to the stock market when it is high, as it has been recently, and get into the market when it is low." Burton Malkiel stated that this correlation may be consistent with an efficient market due to differences in interest rates.

Investors and researchers have disputed the efficient-market hypothesis both empirically and theoretically. Behavioral economists attribute the imperfections in financial markets to a combination of cognitive biases such as overconfidence, overreaction, representative bias, information bias, and various other predictable human errors in reasoning and information processing. These have been researched by psychologists such as Daniel Kahneman, Amos Tversky, Richard Thaler, and Paul Slovic. These errors in reasoning lead most investors to avoid value stocks and buy growth stocks at expensive prices, which allow those who reason correctly to profit from bargains in neglected value stocks and the overreacted selling of growth stocks.

Empirical evidence has been mixed, but has generally not supported strong forms of the efficient-market hypothesis. According to Dreman and Berry, in a 1995 paper, low P/E stocks have greater returns. In an earlier paper Dreman also refuted the assertion by Ray Ball that these higher returns could be attributed to higher beta, whose research had been accepted by efficient market theorists as explaining the anomaly in neat accordance with modern portfolio theory.

One can identify "losers" as stocks that have had poor returns over some number of past years. "Winners" would be those stocks that had high returns over a similar period. The main result of one such study is that losers have much higher average returns than winners over the following period of the same number of years. A later study showed that beta (β) cannot account for this difference in average returns. This tendency of returns to reverse over long horizons (i.e., losers become winners) is yet another contradiction of EMH. Losers would have to have much higher betas than winners in order to justify the return difference. The study showed that the beta difference required to save the EMH is just not there.

Speculative economic bubbles are an obvious anomaly, in that the market often appears to be driven by buyers operating on escalating market sentiment/ irrational exuberance, who take little notice of underlying value. These bubbles are typically followed by an overreaction of frantic selling, allowing shrewd investors to buy stocks at bargain prices. Rational investors have difficulty profiting by shorting irrational bubbles because, as John Maynard Keynes commented, "Markets can stay irrational longer than you can stay solvent." Sudden market crashes as happened on Black Monday in 1987 are mysterious from the perspective of efficient markets, but allowed as a rare *statistical event* under the Weak-form of EMH. One could also argue that if the hypothesis is so weak, it cannot be used in statistical models due to its lack of predictive behavior.

Burton Malkiel, a well-known proponent of the general validity of EMH, has warned that certain emerging markets such as China are not empirically efficient; that the Shanghai and Shenzhen markets, unlike markets in United States, exhibit considerable serial correlation (price trends), non-random walk, and evidence of manipulation.

Behavioral psychology approaches to stock market trading are among some of the more promising alternatives to EMH (and some investment strategies seek to exploit exactly such inefficiencies). But Nobel Laureate co-founder of the program—Daniel Kahneman—announced his skepticism of investors beating the market: "They're [investors] just not going to do it [beat the market]. It's just not going to happen." Indeed defenders of EMH maintain that Behavioral Finance strengthens the case for EMH in that BF highlights biases in individuals and committees and not competitive markets. For example, one prominent finding in Behavioral Finance is that individuals employ hyperbolic discounting. It is palpably true that bonds, mortgages, annuities and other similar financial instruments subject to competitive market forces do not. Any manifestation of hyperbolic discounting in the pricing of these obligations would invite arbitrage thereby quickly eliminating any vestige of individual biases. Similarly, diversification, derivative securities and other hedging strategies assuage if not eliminate potential mispricings from the severe risk-intolerance (loss aversion) of individuals underscored by behavioral finance. On the other hand, economists, behavioral psychologists and mutual fund managers are drawn from the human population and are therefore subject to the biases that behavior lists showcase. By contrast, the price signals in markets are far less subject to individual biases highlighted by the Behavioral Finance program. Richard Thaler has started a fund based on his research on cognitive biases. In a 2008 report he identified complexity and herd behavior as central to the global financial crisis of 2008.

Further empirical work has highlighted the impact transaction costs have on the concept of market efficiency, with much evidence suggesting that any anomalies pertaining to market inefficiencies are the result of a cost benefit analysis made by those willing to incur the cost of acquiring the valuable information in order to trade on it. Additionally the concept of liquidity is a critical component to capturing "inefficiencies" in tests for abnormal returns. Any test of this proposition faces the joint hypothesis problem, where it is impossible to ever test for market efficiency, since to do so requires the use of a measuring stick against which abnormal returns are compared - one cannot know if the market is efficient if one does not know if a model correctly stipulates the required rate of return. Consequently, a situation arises where either the asset pricing model is incorrect or the market is inefficient, but one has no way of knowing which is the case.

A key work on random walk was done in the late 1980s by Profs. Andrew Lo and Craig MacKinlay; they effectively argue that a random walk does not exist, nor ever has. Their paper took almost two years to be accepted by academia and in 1999 they published "A

Non-random Walk Down Wall St." which collects their research papers on the topic up to that time.

Economists Matthew Bishop and Michael Green claim that full acceptance of the hypothesis goes against the thinking of Adam Smith and John Maynard Keynes, who both believed irrational behavior had a real impact on the markets.

Warren Buffett has also argued against EMH, most notably in his 1984 presentation The Superinvestors of Graham-and-Doddsville, saying the preponderance of value investors among the world's best money managers rebuts the claim of EMH proponents that luck is the reason some investors appear more successful than others. As Malkiel has shown, over the 30 years (to 1996) more than two-thirds of professional portfolio managers have been outperformed by the S&P 500 Index (and, more to the point, there is little correlation between those who outperform in one year and those who outperform in the next.)

Late 2000s financial crisis

The financial crisis of 2007–2012 has led to renewed scrutiny and criticism of the hypothesis. Market strategist Jeremy Grantham has stated flatly that the EMH is responsible for the current financial crisis, claiming that belief in the hypothesis caused financial leaders to have a "chronic underestimation of the dangers of asset bubbles breaking". Noted financial journalist Roger Lowenstein blasted the theory, declaring "The upside of the current Great Recession is that it could drive a stake through the heart of the academic nostrum known as the efficient-market hypothesis." Former Federal Reserve chairman Paul Volcker chimed in, saying it's "clear that among the causes of the recent financial crisis was an unjustified faith in rational expectations [and] market efficiencies."

At the International Organization of Securities Commissions annual conference, held in June 2009, the hypothesis took center stage. Martin Wolf, the chief economics commentator for the Financial Times, dismissed the hypothesis as being a useless way to examine how markets function in reality. Paul McCulley, managing director of PIMCO, was less extreme in his criticism, saying that the hypothesis had not failed, but was "seriously flawed" in its neglect of human nature.

The financial crisis has led Richard Posner, a prominent judge, University of Chicago law professor, and innovator in the field of Law and Economics, to back away from the hypothesis and express some degree of belief in Keynesian economics. Posner accused some of his Chicago School colleagues of being "asleep at the switch", saying that "the movement to deregulate the financial industry went too far by exaggerating the resilience - the self healing powers - of laissez-faire capitalism." Others, such as Fama himself, said that the hypothesis held up well during the crisis and that the markets were a casualty of the recession, not the cause of it. Despite this, Fama has conceded that "poorly informed investors could theoretically lead the market astray" and that stock prices could become "somewhat irrational" as a result.

Critics have suggested that financial institutions and corporations have been able to reduce the efficiency of financial markets by creating private information and reducing the accuracy of conventional disclosures, and by developing new and complex products which are challenging for most market participants to evaluate and correctly price.

*****

Here is the most significant part of the above article, "There are three major versions of the hypothesis: "weak", "semi-strong", and "strong". The weak-form EMH claims that prices on traded assets (*e.g.,* stocks, bonds, or property) already reflect all past publicly available information. The semi-strong-form EMH claims both that prices reflect all publicly available information and that prices instantly change to reflect new public information. The strong-form EMH additionally claims that prices instantly reflect even hidden or "insider" information. Critics have blamed the belief in rational markets for much of the late-2000s financial crisis. In response, proponents of the hypothesis have stated that market efficiency does not mean having no uncertainty about the future, that market efficiency is a simplification of the world which may not always hold true, and that the market is practically efficient for investment purposes for most individuals."

To me, this is a silly theory because it has been proven unreliable but still they cling to this, which in turn disrupts the marketplace. I will leave it to my readers to make their own judgement but theories such as EMH need to be removed.

Chapter 5 – Summary & Conclusions

Behavioral Finance Psychology - Bias, Emotion, & Overconfidence is an in-depth personal resource that reveals the causes behind perception investing, behavioral finance, behavioral finance investors, behavioral finance psychology, behavioral finance theory, behavioral investing, and wealth management. Using systematic and proven behavioral science, the author reveals why stock markets fluctuate seemingly at the whim of investors and for no rational reason. Some of the topics addressed in this book include the "noise trader theory," Efficient Market Hypothesis (EMH) and current research into psychological behavior of investors including serial correlation patterns in stock price data and behavioral finance biases.

Behavioral Finance Psychology - Bias, Emotion, & Overconfidence discusses the most essential elements of behavioral finance, including psychological concepts, behavioral biases, behavioral aspects of asset pricing, asset allocation, market prices, investor behavior, corporate managerial behavior, and social influences.

Chapter 1 offers a brief treatise on behavioral science and the mechanism of the human mind and how it governs behavior.

Chapter 2 is all about "Perception Investing" and how emotions drive the marketplace.

I then introduced you to the "Noise Trader Theory" which is very real but often discounted in the financial marketplace.

And last, I introduced you to the silly "Efficient Market Hypothesis" and it is dumb!!!

Now I have a special gift for you…read on…

I Have a Special Gift for My Readers

I appreciate my readers for without them I am just another author attempting to make a difference. If my book has made a favorable impression please leave me an honest review. Thank you in advance for you participation.

My readers and I have in common a passion for the written word as well as the desire to learn and grow from books.

My special offer to you is a massive ebook library that I have compiled over the years. It contains hundreds of fiction and non-fiction ebooks in Adobe Acrobat PDF format as well as the Greek classics and old literary classics too.

In fact, this library is so massive to completely download the entire library will require over 5 GBs open on your desktop.

Use the link below and scan all of the ebooks in the library. You can select the ebooks you want individually or download the entire library.

The link below does not expire after a given time period so you are free to return for more books rather than clog your desktop. And feel free to give the link to your friends who enjoy reading too.

I thank you for reading my book and hope if you are pleased that you will leave me an honest review so that I can improve my work and or write books that appeal to your interests.

Okay, here is the link…

http://tinyurl.com/special-readers-promo

PS: If you wish to reach me personally for any reason you may simply write to mailto:support@epubwealth.com.

I answer all of my emails so rest assured I will respond.

Meet the Author

Dr. Leland Benton is Director of Applied Web Info, a holding company for ePubWealth.com, a leading ePublisher company based in Utah. With over 21,000 resellers in over 22-countries, ePubWealth.com is a leader in ePublishing, book promotion, and ebook marketing.

As the creator and author of "The ePubWealth Program," Leland teaches up-and-coming authors the ins-and-outs of today's ePublishing world. He has assisted hundreds of authors make it big in the ePublishing world.

Leland also created a series of external book promotion programs and teaches authors how to promote their books using external marketing sources.

Leland is also the Managing Director of Applied Mind Sciences, the company's mind research unit and Chief Forensics Investigator for the company's ForensicsNation unit. He is active in privacy rights through the company's PrivacyNations unit and is an expert in survival planning and disaster relief through the company's SurvivalNations unit.

Leland resides in Southern Utah.

Visit some of his websites
http://appliedmindsciences.com/
http://appliedwebinfo.com/
http://BookbuilderPLUS.com

http://embarrassingproblemsfix.com/
http://www.epubwealth.com/
http://forensicsnation.com/
http://neternatives.com/
http://privacynations.com/
http://survivalnations.com/
http://thebentonkitchen.com
http://theolegions.org

www.ingramcontent.com/pod-product-compliance
Lightning Source LLC
Chambersburg PA
CBHW051727170526
45167CB00002B/831